10 festive classics for
FLUTE AND PIANO with ECD

Arranged by Richard Harris

FLUTE PART

Contents

	page	track
Frosty the snowman	2	1
Walking in the air	3	2
Let it snow! Let it snow! Let it snow!	4	3
Last Christmas	5	4
Jingle bells	6	5
The Christmas Song (Chestnuts roasting on an open fire)	7	6
Rockin' around the Christmas tree	8	7
Do they know it's Christmas?	9	8
Rockin' robin	10	9
Rudolph the red-nosed reindeer	11	10

Using the Enhanced CD (ECD)

A PDF of the piano accompaniment is included on the ECD for you to print out as necessary. A single print out of this musical work only is authorised. (This work includes copyright material owned by parties other than Faber Music, and unauthorised copies will constitute an infringement of the rights of such parties as well as those of Faber Music.)
In order to view this file, you will need Adobe Reader, which is available for free download from www.adobe.com

The text paper used in this publication is a virgin fibre product that is manufactured in the UK to ISO 14001 standards. The wood fibre used is only sourced from managed forests using sustainable forestry principles. This paper is 100% recyclable.

© 2008 by Faber Music Ltd
First published in 2008 by Faber Music Ltd
Music processed by Donald Sheppard
Cover design by Kenosha
Printed in England by Caligraving Ltd
All rights reserved

ISBN10: 0-571-53150-4
EAN13: 978-0-571-53150-9

Backings created and engineered by Ben Tompsett
Produced by Leigh Rumsey
℗ 2008 Faber Music Ltd © 2008 Faber Music Ltd

Frosty the snowman

Words and Music by Steve Nelson
and Jack Rollins

BACKING TRACK 2

Walking in the air
Theme from *The Snowman*

Words and Music by Howard Blake

4

Let it snow! Let it snow! Let it snow!

BACKING TRACK 3

Words by Sammy Cahn
Music by Jule Styne

Last Christmas

Words and Music by George Michael

Jingle bells

BACKING TRACK 5

Words and Music by James Pierpont

© 2008 Faber Music Ltd

The Christmas Song
(Chestnuts roasting on an open fire)

Words and Music by Mel Tormé
and Robert Wells

8

BACKING TRACK [7]

Rockin' around the Christmas tree

Words and Music by Johnny Marks

Do they know it's Christmas?

Words and Music by Bob Geldof
and Midge Ure

Rockin' robin

Words and Music by Jimmie Thomas

© 1958 Unichappell Music Inc
Carlin Music Corp

BACKING TRACK 10

Rudolph the red-nosed reindeer

Words and Music by Johnny Marks

The Faber Music 'PLAY' Series

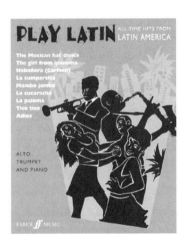

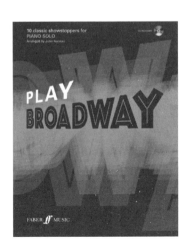

Play Ballads (flute and piano)	ISBN 0-571-52002-2
Play Ballads (clarinet and piano)	ISBN 0-571-51999-7
Play Ballads (alto saxophone and piano)	ISBN 0-571-52008-1
Play Ballads (trumpet and piano)	ISBN 0-571-51996-2
Play Gershwin (violin and piano)	ISBN 0-571-51622-X
Play Gershwin (cello and piano)	ISBN 0-571-51623-8
Play Gershwin (clarinet and piano)	ISBN 0-571-51754-4
Play Gershwin (alto saxophone and piano)	ISBN 0-571-51755-2
Play Jazztime (violin and piano)	ISBN 0-571-51908-3
Play Jazztime (flute and piano)	ISBN 0-571-51822-2
Play Jazztime (clarinet and piano)	ISBN 0-571-51821-4
Play Jazztime (alto saxophone and piano)	ISBN 0-571-51909-1
Play Jazztime (trumpet and piano)	ISBN 0-571-52045-6
Play Latin (piano)	ISBN 0-571-51895-8
Play Latin (flute and piano)	ISBN 0-571-51771-4
Play Latin (clarinet and piano)	ISBN 0-571-51772-2
Play Latin (alto saxophone and piano)	ISBN 0-571-52047-2
Play Latin (trumpet and piano)	ISBN 0-571-52046-4
Play Showtime (cello and piano)	ISBN 0-571-51851-6
Play Showtime Book 1 (violin and piano)	ISBN 0-571-51588-6
Play Showtime Book 2 (violin and piano)	ISBN 0-571-51530-4
Play Showtime Book 1 (alto saxophone and piano)	ISBN 0-571-51616-5
Play Showtime Book 2 (alto saxophone and piano)	ISBN 0-571-51606-8
Play Showtime Book 1 (trumpet and piano)	ISBN 0-571-51615-7
Play Showtime Book 2 (trumpet and piano)	ISBN 0-571-51605-X
Play Soul (flute and piano with CD)	ISBN 0-571-52460-5
Play Soul (clarinet and piano with CD)	ISBN 0-571-52461-3
Play Soul (alto saxophone and piano with CD)	ISBN 0-571-52462-1
Play Soul (trumpet and piano with CD)	ISBN 0-571-52463-X
Play Broadway (flute and piano with CD)	ISBN 0-571-52631-4
Play Broadway (clarinet and piano with CD)	ISBN 0-571-52632-2
Play Broadway (alto saxophone and piano with CD)	ISBN 0-571-52633-0
Play Broadway (trumpet and piano with CD)	ISBN 0-571-52634-9
Play Broadway (violin and piano with CD)	ISBN 0-571-52635-7
Play Broadway (piano with CD)	ISBN 0-571-52748-5
Play Hollywood (flute and piano with ECD)	ISBN 0-571-52822-8
Play Hollywood (clarinet and piano with ECD)	ISBN 0-571-52823-6
Play Hollywood (alto saxophone and piano with ECD)	ISBN 0-571-52824-4
Play Hollywood (trumpet and piano with ECD)	ISBN 0-571-52825-2
Play Hollywood (piano with CD)	ISBN 0-571-52826-0
Play Christmas (flute and piano with ECD)	ISBN 0-571-53150-4
Play Christmas (clarinet and piano with ECD)	ISBN 0-571-53151-2
Play Christmas (alto saxophone with ECD)	ISBN 0-571-53152-0
Play Christmas (trumpet and piano with ECD)	ISBN 0-571-53153-9
Play Christmas (violin and piano with ECD)	ISBN 0-571-53154-7
Play Christmas (piano with CD)	ISBN 0-571-53155-5